SOUTH

SOUTH

BILL WEEMS

TEXT BY JOHN EGERTON

GRAPHIC ARTS CENTER PUBLISHING COMPANY

This book is dedicated to Robert E. Gilka who gave me the chance to begin and the courage to continue. — *Bill Weems.*

THE SOUTH

International Standard Book Number: 0-932575-32-3
Library of Congress Catalog Number: # 87-081210
© MCMLXXXVII by Graphic Arts Center Publishing Company
P.O. Box 10306 • Portland, Oregon 97210 • (503) 226-2402
Editor-in-Chief: Douglas A. Pfeiffer
Cartographer: Tom Patterson
Design: Cargill and Associates, Inc., Atlanta, Georgia
Printed in Japan

Introduction

I was born in Georgia. I grew up in North Carolina, hiked through the Blue Ridge Mountains, played on the Outer Banks, and swam the cool, slow streams of the Piedmont. Later I moved to Charleston and dropped my son into his legacy of Southern heritage.

When I began work on this book many months ago, I thought I knew the South. Yet the more I traveled, visiting Southerners in their special part of America, the more I realized I was wrong. I didn't know the South at all. Unknown to me, there were new experiences waiting every day in a cotton field, on a riverboat, or in some newly discovered corner of a small old town. There isn't just one South—there are many, each quite different from all others, and each with its own remarkable character. Indeed, it is the diversity of the people who share such a strong Southern identity that has left its deep impression on me.

A Tangier Island oysterman and an Atlanta stockbroker, an Arkansas rice farmer and a Florida livestock owner, a Kentucky coal miner and an Alabama shipyard worker—all have lifestyles so distinct and separate from one another that they could well be living in different countries. Yet, everywhere I went, I sensed a common bond, a kinship with one another, a commitment to being Southern.

The richness of the Southern landscape is stunning. From the Dry Tortuga islands only sixty miles off Havana to the peak of Mount Mitchell, the highest point east of the Mississippi River, the land offers an unending variety of sea islands, pristine estuaries, coastal dunes, sparkling rivers, soft rolling hills, high mountains, and endless forests. It is the land that bonds the Southern people. They are as one in their communion with their earth, as inseparably tied to it as to their families and to their history. More than any other region of America, the South is...itself.

Yet, even as I write, the South is in motion. Although the Southern countryside remains quiet, Southern cities are forward-looking, bustling, modern. The new Southerners from New York and Michigan mingle with the old. Couples formerly of Vermont and New Jersey have resettled throughout the Southern states, bringing new perspectives and new enthusiasm. Businesses from Belgium and Japan fill Southern valleys and introduce new ways of doing things.

Today, the South is a dynamic region poised carefully between the richness of its past and the unknown excitement of the future.

Page 1: *Audubon Park, New Orleans, Louisiana.* Pages 2/3: *Farm land near Sinking Creek, Virginia.* Page 4/5: *Tuckasegee River near Cullowhee, North Carolina.* Page 6: *Pink dogwood, Ozarks, near Silver Hill, Arkansas.* Page 7: *Buffalo River near Dillards Ferry, Arkansas.*

Opposite page (above): *Red spruce glen, Mount Mitchell, North Carolina.* Opposite page (below): *Tidal pools, De Bordieu Island, South Carolina.* This page: *Magnolia blossoms, Vicksburg, Mississippi.*

The Land

It is daybreak in the South.

Knee-deep in the rushing waters of a crystalline mountain brook, a trout fisherman in the Arkansas Ozarks casts for his breakfast.

Thundering over a dirt track in the lush Kentucky Bluegrass, a thoroughbred colt responds to its rider's commands in a race against the wind.

Lost in thought, a lone visitor to Roanoke Island on the North Carolina coast ponders the English attempt to establish a colony there in 1587.

With a squadron of seagulls in its wake, a Gulf Coast shrimp boat chugs out of Apalachicola Bay in the Florida Panhandle, bound for a day of fishing.

At the edge of a cotton field in south Alabama, a farmer rubs rich black dirt between his callused fingers and surveys his dew-drenched crop.

Over a flickering campfire in the east Tennessee hills, an early-rising cook savors the mingled fragrances of boiling coffee, wood smoke, and springtime.

Pages 12/13: *Clingmans Dome, Tennessee, with Great Smoky Mountains beyond.* Opposite page: *Near Hazeltop Mountain, Shenandoah National Park, Virginia.* This page: *Before the storm, near Tifton, Georgia.*

These are Southern people on the land, with the elements, in nature—looking, listening, feeling the pulse, searching for the signs. They have been here for centuries, for longer than the span of recorded memory. In every state, every season, and every circumstance, Southerners have always been close to the land.

Imagine how this Eden must have looked to Tecumseh's and Sequoyah's ancestors, those aboriginal hunters, fishers, and farmers whose eyes first saw the glory of it thousands of years ago.

Or imagine how it looked to Juan Ponce de León, sailing northward in the ink-blue waters of the Atlantic in 1513 and seeing off the port side a narrow strip of white sand and a dense thicket of lowland greenery that turned out to be not another West Indies island but the east coast of Florida.

The scouts went back with spellbinding tales of excitement, and others soon came to see for themselves: Hernando de Soto, for example. In 1539, he landed in

Tampa Bay on the west coast of Florida and led a small company of soldiers on a four-year exploration of the vast interior wilderness of North America's southeastern region. Surely they were awed to speechlessness by the wild beauty of it all.

The parade quickened. One May morning in 1607, Captain Christopher Newport landed with a handful of sea-weary Englishmen on a marshy peninsula of the James River and established there a beachhead of the Virginia Colony. Still later, in 1682, the French explorer René Robert Cavelier, Sieur de la Salle, descended the Mississippi River to the Gulf of Mexico by canoe. Imagine the wonders they beheld.

These were the adventurers, the pathfinders, the intrepid astronauts, and the moonwalkers of their time; they were sojourners in a land of deep mystery, pilgrims to the South before there was a South. What they saw in the territory bordered on the north by the Ohio River and on the west by the watershed of the Mississippi was a half-million square miles of enormous geographical diversity and stunning primeval beauty. From the beginning and all along, it has lingered in the memory as a singular land, a place apart.

For more than three centuries after Ponce de León's journey to Florida, the South lacked a clear identity. To the first European explorers, it was thought of simply as a part of America, an undifferentiated mass of wilderness territory ripe for colonial exploitation. Later, to the coastal settlers, it was the West—the land beyond—and it retained that designation until Texas and California and the "true West" became part of the United States in the middle of the nineteenth century. Throughout that time, as

This page: *Central Florida sunrise.* Opposite page (above): *Snail tracks, Natchez Trace, Mississippi.* Opposite page (below): *Boneyard Ossabaw Island, Georgia.*

the South was acquiring countless internal appellations—names for its states, its communities, its natural features, and its institutions—it was also bonding its character and personality to the land and sea, to the mountains and plains, to the rivers and streams, and to the seasons.

The physical endowments that nature bestowed upon the South were rich beyond counting, so rich that the common reaction of the pathfinders to what they found here could only have been amazement. Who among them could have anticipated virgin forests as vast as these, or mountain ranges as long and rugged as the Appalachians, or lowland swamps as large as the Florida Everglades, or rivers as mighty as the Mississippi? Who could have guessed how varied and plenteous the edible flora and fauna would be—the animals and birds and fishes, the fruits and nuts and berries, the wild vegetables and the ones that soon would be cultivated? Who would have believed how hot and sultry the summers could be in the lower South, or how pleasantly mild the winters?

Magnitude and quantity characterized the natural blessings of the region. The great rivers included not just the Mississippi and the Ohio but the Arkansas, the Tennessee, the James, the Savannah, the St. Johns, and many others. In addition to the Appalachian Mountains, there were also the Smokies, the Blue Ridge, the Alleghenies, the Cumberlands, and the Ozarks. Besides the Everglades, there were such lowland features as Georgia's Okefenokee Swamp, Louisiana's Atchafalaya Basin, and the sprawling delta flatlands of Mississippi and Arkansas. Along the Atlantic and Gulf coasts there were subregions that stood out one from another: Virginia's Eastern Shore, North Carolina's Outer Banks, South Carolina's Low Country, Georgia's Sea Islands, Florida's Keys and Panhandle, the coastal strips of Alabama and Mississippi, and the bayous of Louisiana.

These natural features were present when the first Europeans arrived,

and they have remained in place as permanent beauty marks, jewels in the Southern crown. Things do change, of course—cities rise up along waterfronts and at crossroad junctions, people migrate in and out, technology continually transforms the systems of communication and transportation and alters the ways people live and work. But in spite of urban and industrial growth and all the other contemporary manifestations of change, the South is more clearly defined by its natural assets than by man-made ones; even in its cities a hint of the country remains. The rural and agricultural patterns of life may inevitably give way to the pace and sophistication of the modern world, but the call of the outdoors still echoes, and the most powerful refrains in the siren song of the senses are also the most familiar and traditional.

In the South, the sights and sounds that trigger recollection and the sensations of smell and taste and touch that stir the memory are deeply rooted in the land and in nature. A sunrise in the Smokies, a sunset on the Gulf, a full moon over the Atlantic—these are dramatic images that never lose their power to inspire. The hushed whisper of the wind in the pines, the symphony of birdsong at daybreak, the soothing rush and tinkle of a cold mountain stream—these are sounds that no Southern nature lover ever tires of hearing. The heady fragrance of orange blossoms, the juicy sweetness of a ripe peach, the gentle softness of beach sand sifting through the fingers—these are sensuous pleasures that no amount of repetition can dull.

Out of the hard red clay of the hill country, the sandy loam of the coastal lowlands, and the rich black alluvial soil of the deltas, generations of Southerners have harvested abundant quantities of seasonal produce—spring asparagus and strawberries and bibb lettuce, summer sweet corn and field peas and tomatoes, fall apples and peanuts and pecans, winter citrus and turnip greens and collards. For beauty and fragrance, there is a perpetual showcase of blossoms that seem almost synonymous with the South: dogwoods and azaleas, camellias and magnolias, wisteria and crepe myrtle, and rhododendron and mountain laurel. The ancient sentinels are gone from the forests, but younger stands of hardwoods and evergreens have risen in their place, dense enough in some bosky precincts to blot out the summer sun. The diverse plenitude of hickory and ash and oak, maple and poplar and gum, locust and beech, and countless others fills the autumn woods with fiery blazes of color.

No one can decipher the mystical rhythms of the calendar; like ocean currents, the seasons move according to their own unseen clock, bringing with them flood and drought, fire and ice, hurricanes, tornadoes, and heat waves.

Against such power there is no defense, only grudging compliance. Southern stewards of the land know the futility of resistance; they can only wait on the weather, bending with its winds or bowing to its soaking rains and scorching sunshine—understanding all the while that only time can balance the ever-turning wheel of deliverance.

And the land remains, always the land. Institutions rise and fall, people come and go, the weather constantly changes, but the land holds on. It is the literal and figurative ground of Southern life, the bedrock of Southern being. Some unthinking tenants may assault it with blight and pollution—contaminate its soils, burn its forests, stain its healing waters with refuse, fill the air above it with noxious poisons—but the land survives. It was here before the ancestors of Tecumseh and Sequoyah arrived, and from every indication, it will be present still when the human parade has run its course.

This page: *Rhododendron, Grandfather Mountain, North Carolina.*
Opposite page: *Church building near Deals Gap, North Carolina.*

Pages 20/21: *Albermarle Sound, North Carolina.* Pages 22/23: *Cumberland Gap, Kentucky, looking toward Kentucky and Virginia.* This page: *Camellia, Lakeland, Florida.* Opposite page: *Snowy egret, De Bordieu Island, South Carolina*

Pages 26/27: *Windsor
Mansion ruins, near Port
Gibson, Mississippi.* This
page: *Country road near
Clemson, South Carolina.*
Opposite page: *Summer
rainstorm in fields near
Port Gibson, Mississippi.*

Pages 30/31: *Cades Cove,
Tennessee.* This page:
*Otters near Georgetown,
South Carolina.*
Opposite page: *Canoeing
in the Florida Everglades.*

This page: *Hang gliding, Jockeys Ridge, North Carolina.*

Pages 36/37:
Steamboating on Mississippi
River above Vicksburg,
Mississippi. Opposite
page: *Atchafalaya Swamp,*
Louisiana. This page
(above): *Cajun crawfisher-*
man, St. Martinsville,
Louisiana. This page
(below): *Cooked crawfish*
dinner, Atchafalya
Swamp, Louisiana.

Pages 40/41: *Barn near Mountain View, Arkansas.* This page: *Scarlet tanager near Rocky Fort, Tennessee.* Opposite page: *Wild ponies, Okracoke Island, North Carolina.* Pages 44/45: *New River landscape near Mouth of Wilson, Virginia.*

The Workplace

Their hands tell the story. Weathered by wind and water, by earth and sun, they show themselves to be tough but also supple, like good leather work gloves. They range in color through shades of ebony and pecan and peach. Whether long and sinewy or short and thick, whether neatly manicured or with dirt beneath the nails, they bespeak power and strength. The nimble adroitness of long experience, the jagged scars of combat with tools and machines, the folds and creases of lengthening time—all are there on display to be read like an open book, like chapters of an autobiography.

These are the hands of hard-working people. They can be as solid as a clenched fist, as soft as a consoling hug, as expressive as an honest face. They are the hands that found the South, explored it, farmed it, built it. Now, as the South takes on a different appearance, a modern character, it is these old hands that reveal the labor it took—and still takes—to make a society on the land.

After name and address—the genealogy and the geography—it is work that describes and defines Southern people most clearly, especially in the rural areas and small towns. The questions a native puts to a stranger are tellingly familiar: What is your name? Who are your people? Where are they from? What do they do? The answers to the last query are much more varied now than they used to be, back in the days when agriculture and related occupations engaged a large majority of the people.

What Southerners do today is very much the same as what Americans elsewhere do. The work is as much cerebral as it is manual, as much on paper, computer screens, or television monitors as it is outdoors on the land, so the hands no longer tell the story as they once did.

But in the long evolution of Southern labor from the prehistoric fishing, hunting, and farming skills of the Indians to the futuristic marvel of high technology that now is becoming a routine fixture in the workplace, there always has been a certain style or quality or character, a certain attitude, that seems to typify the way people in the region go about their business. It might be an overstatement to say there is such a thing as a distinct and definable Southern work ethic, but there are certainly habits and practices that working people in this corner of the country have followed for a very long time.

From the beginning, the work itself was arduous, back-breaking, and interminable. Clearing the land and farming it, building the towns and cities, raising the children, feeding and caring for the

Pages 46/47: *Eel fisherman, Pamlico River North Carolina.* Opposite page: *Mountain men, Mabel Community near Boone, North Carolina.*

people—all required unremitting labor. For two and a half centuries, much of it was slave labor, a fact that influenced the work habits of both black and white Southerners throughout that time and for well over a century after slavery was abolished. During and after slavery, though, people of both races were constantly up against a far more physically demanding labor requirement than they are today, and the sort of leisure time that most people now enjoy routinely was unheard of then for all but a privileged few.

And beyond the work, there was the weather: in some parts bitterly cold in winter, always a veritable furnace of suffocating heat and humidity in the dog days of summer. Southerners became acclimated to the extremes, learned to live with them and work in them, or they left, there being no other choice open to them. Sometimes puzzled outsiders have watched Southerners at work—deliberate, methodical, unhurried—and incorrectly concluded that they were lazy and unproductive; on the contrary, the experience of generations has taught them the most sensible and efficient way to perform hard work in hot weather.

Living so close to the very heartbeat of nature, feeling its breath upon the skin, inhaling its earthy perfumes, hearing its myriad cries and whispers, Southerners in earlier times learned above all

to respect the natural order, even when they could neither predict it nor comprehend it. The pathfinders and those who followed them came to understand the wisdom of observing the moon, the tides, the currents, the rainfall, and the signs of seasonal evolution. Directly or indirectly, almost all of them worked somewhere in the food chain. Now, removed though they are from such close association with the life of the land, most native Southerners nevertheless have an appreciation for it, and it keeps many of them attached, however tenuously, to traditional feelings about work and leisure.

Animals are another reminder of the mystical call of nature. Some of the farm livestock, the beasts of burden—mules, horses, and oxen—once were so essential as to be considered part of the work force. The rest contributed in various ways—eggs from the chickens, milk and cheese and butter from the cows, wool from the sheep, lard from the hogs,

This page: *Nissan factory, Smyrna, Tennessee.*
Opposite page: *Spools in a textile mill, Spartanburg, South Carolina.*

manufacturers, shipbuilders, chemical companies, and the like.

Of all the areas of work and play to hold the attention of Southerners past and present, probably none could be thought of as more representative or symbolic of the regional character than music. As a bridge between the traditional and the contemporary, between the hands, the heart, and the head, music spans the many avenues of Southern feeling and expression. The vocal and instrumental music of the South is a regional treasure combining many skills—storytelling, songwriting, instrument making, and performing. It is creative art, it is work—and it is, quite literally, play. It has been embedded in the soul of the South for longer than anyone can remember, longer than there has been a South, and it is as diverse and as singular as the people themselves.

In Indian cultures, music played an important ceremonial role. Then the field songs of the slaves gave rise to the first indigenous American art form: the blues. Gospel music was born in Southern churches. Folk, country, and bluegrass music originated in the hills of Virginia and North Carolina, Kentucky

and meat from them all. Pets, particularly dogs and cats, have always been highly visible and important in Southern households. As for wild animals, hunters and fishermen have pursued them avidly throughout the centuries of habitation in the region. Even now, it is not unheard of for a company in the South to give workers a day off on the first day of a hunting season.

Some traditional occupations do remain, of course. Farming, for all its tribulations in recent times, is still a major industry in every Southern state, and the agricultural support enterprises, including everything from seed companies to farm implement distributors, are also substantial. The hands are still important, too, in the arts and crafts, in furniture making, in the diversified fishing businesses, and in the heavy industries that have come into the region in recent years—automotive and Tennessee, Georgia and Arkansas. New Orleans is the first home of jazz, and even rock and roll, an invention of the mid-twentieth century, counts several Southern musical geniuses in its inner circle of patron saints. It is no exaggeration to say that the birthplace of American music is here in the states of the southeastern corner of the country.

The workplace, in this interpretation, is everywhere to be found, from church sanctuaries to highway honky-tonks. Performers and listeners alike understand the nature of this creative activity, and they approach it with respect. They are familiar with the instruments. They know the words and the music.

There is a mood of celebration, of expectancy. Finally, the lights are dimmed, a quiet descends, and the music begins. As the evening progresses, those present—the workers and the watchers—lose all sense of time; each alone and all together, they are transported to other rooms, other places of the heart and soul.

Standing outside this marvelous phenomenon, we watch with pleasure and wonder, seeing the faces and hearing the sounds. And if we are very observant, we notice the hands: aged and seasoned, knowing, gifted, commanding the tools they hold with dignity and grace. These are the hands of hard-working Southern people, preserving and extending the life of their land.

Opposite page:
Cotton harvest near
Dothan, Alabama.

Pages 54/55: *Industrial
sector, Savannah, Georgia.*
Opposite page: *Raking
the mountaintop near
Burnsville, North Carolina.*
This page: *Pulling
tobacco pickers, Wilson,
North Carolina.*

Opposite page: *Ship
welder, Bender Shipyard,
Mobile, Alabama.* This
page: *Ship building yards,
Pascagoula, Mississippi.*

Pages 60/61: *Oil drilling platform, South Mobile Bay, Alabama.* This page: *Between offices, Atlanta, Georgia.* Opposite page: *Loading soybeans for export, Port of Mobile, Alabama.*

Opposite page: *Old-time crabber on Moon River, Georgia.* This page: *Scientist at Centers for Disease Control, Atlanta, Georgia.*

The People

Who are the Southerners?

Romantic novels and movies and television have projected a long line of stereotyped images in answer to the question. Out of the antebellum era came goateed plantation colonels, fluttering ladies in crinolines, and happy slaves singing in the cotton fields. In modern times, a different but no less banal and artificial cast of characters has been featured: dim-witted hillbillies and mountaineers, red-neck sheriffs, sweet-voiced beauty queens, and tobacco-chewing good old boys.

Reality brings a much broader and deeper array of people into focus—not distorted, one-dimensional caricatures, but a congeries of humanity. Today's Southerners range across the spectrum of age, race, residence, occupation, and income. They are men and women, native-born and adopted, who sometimes seem as different from one another as they are unlike people elsewhere—and yet, at the same time, many of them have in common certain manners and habits, certain ways of speaking, and certain traits of personality that mark them unmistakably as Southerners.

It is both their differences and their similarities that make them interesting. The people of the South often stand apart from their fellow Americans—more markedly, perhaps, than do North-erners or Easterners or Westerners. For better and worse, through generations of fabricated images and stark realities, Southerners somehow have managed to preserve remnants of their regional iden-tity as individuals and as a people, in spite of the gradual emergence of a look-alike culture across the nation as a whole.

Within the region, the simple fact of diversity is a myth-shattering surprise to many non-Southerners who have pic-

tured the people in clear-cut terms of white and black. Indeed, Anglo-Saxons and Afro-Americans do comprise the two largest segments of the population, as they always have, but there are other nationalities and ethnic groups whose presence has been clearly visible and whose influence is still felt. The imprint of the Spanish in Florida and the French in Louisiana is primary and indelible. The German heritage in North Carolina and Kentucky has been substantial, too, and the same can be said of the Italians and Greeks in several of the Southern states. East Europeans have been less numerous, but they still have made

Pages 66/67: *Dress parade, The Citadel, Charleston, South Carolina.* Opposite page: *Farmers Market, Raleigh, North Carolina.* This page: *After the Peachtree Road Race, Atlanta, Georgia.*

important contributions to Southern culture, as have Mexicans; and even Chinese have lived in the Mississippi Delta for more than a hundred years. In recent times, the influx of Hispanics from Central and South America and refugees from Southeast Asia has further broadened the South's ethnic diversity.

In the realm of religion, a similar pattern can be found. From colonial times to the present, it has been not just Protestants but Catholics and Jews as well who have worshipped here. Even among the Protestants, the major denominations were complemented early and often by such historic religious communities as the Moravians, the Quakers and the Shakers, the Amish and the Mennonites.

Beyond ethnic and religious diversity, the South has shown a curious acceptance of one particular kind of social diversity—namely, a general accommodation of eccentric characters. For reasons that have never been clear, eccentricity has always seemed to thrive in the region, particularly in the arena of politics and other spectator sports.

The fact that diversity did not breed tolerance is one of the ironic twists of Southern history; intolerance—racial, ethnic, religious, and social—was deeply ingrained in the region until the upheavals of the mid-twentieth century took place, and manifestations of the old reaction still surface occasionally.

But the traits of character that persist in Southern culture, giving the region and its people their distinctiveness, are essentially positive. The bonds of kinship and friendship, of custom and tradition and ritual, are not confined within racial or religious or social boundaries. Southerners of every description show deep feeling for the unifying occasions of social exchange, be they barbecues, fish fries, and dinners on the ground, or weddings, funerals, and homecomings on the land.

In their heart of hearts, Southerners are social beings; their energizing source of power is talk, expression, and verbal exchange. Until architecture changed after World War II and the magnets of air conditioning and television drew people off the porches and into the parlors, families spent many a summer evening talking in the dark. News, gossip, history, humor, fiction, and even poetry were on the agenda, and music occasionally spiced the fare. There was porch talk in the summer, hearth talk in the winter, and table talk and pillow talk anytime; little wonder, then, that so many Southerners are skilled listeners, renowned talkers, even gifted writers.

This page: *New Southerners, New Orleans, Louisiana.*
Opposite page: *Deckhand on Delta Queen steamship, Mississippi.*

"In the North they tell jokes," said Robert Penn Warren, who has gone from his non-urban Kentucky and Tennessee roots to world fame as a poet and novelist, "but in the South, at least in the South of that pre-television time, they told tales—elaborate, winding, wandering creations that might never wear out, stories full of human perception and subtlety, told with a richness of language and expression." It was, said Warren, "a regional difference." Talk in the porch age, he concluded, was "a Southern gift that springs from the pores of the society."

It is easy to trace the extension of that gift of words from the level of casual conversation into other dimensions of Southern life. Out of all proportion to their numbers, people who were raised in this region have gained prominence as novelists, poets, teachers, preachers, journalists, historians, lawyers, judges, politicians—and all of those professions require the same sort of listening and talking skills that long evenings on the porch provided.

Expression—verbal, written, and musical—is a Southern hallmark. If it is correct to generalize about taciturn New Englanders or Western men of few words, it is equally correct to speak of garrulous Southerners. Fired with imagination, inspired by their own rhetoric and that of others, they are forever talking and singing, preaching and praying, crying and laughing.

A gradual flattening of regional accents has been taking place across the United States over the past quarter-century or so. Television is probably the main contributing factor, valuing as it does the sort of neutral, standard, unaccented speaking style that is easily understood in all regions of the country. Against this trend, Southern voices have shown flashes of persistence. There are dozens of distinctive subregional accents within the South; some of them, particularly in rural areas, seem hardly to have changed at all over the years. In the Mississippi Delta, in the Cajun country of Louisiana, in the Ozarks and the Appalachians, in the South Carolina Low Country, and along Virginia's Eastern Shore, the lyrical cadence of local speech reverberates with language that echoes a distant past. In these rich voices of black and white Southerners,

there is at once a subtle distinguishing quality that can be heard from one location to another—and at the same time a general style and substance that marks the speakers as Southerners.

Eventually, inevitably, the powerful currents of contemporary culture may erase the most salient features of regionalism in this diverse land—but if and when that happens, the South and its people may be the last to give up their claims to distinction.

Who are the Southerners? Whoever is self-consciously, self-confidently, self-evidently so; whoever claims the title and affirms the description; whoever bears the signs.

With a feeling of comfort and a sense of belonging, the people of the South return time and time again to their chosen land and to the familiar places of life and work that fill their dreams and stir their memories. In ceremonial circles, they gather and join hands with those who never left, the sons and daughters whose stewardship of the land, of the homeplace, and of the workplace has been continuous. With all their human diversity and variety, they are nonetheless one, united by history and myth and the overpowering presence of their place on earth. One and all, once and always, they are the Southerners.

Opposite page:
Retired stockbroker,
Mobile, Alabama.

This page: *The Juliette
Gordon Lowe Home,
Savannah, Georgia.*
Opposite page:
*Grande dame of
Flinthill, Virginia.*

Pages 76/77: *Masters
Golf Tournament,
Augusta, Georgia.* Pages
78/79: *Intracoastal Sail-
boat Regatta, Wassaw
Sound, Georgia.* Oppo-
site page: *Farm Couple,
Wilson, North Carolina.*
This page: *Korean
Baptist Church picnic,
Audubon Park, New
Orleans, Louisiana.*

This page: *Confederate Forces, Battle of Manassas reenactment, Virginia.*
Opposite page: *Union Forces, Battle of Manassas reenactment, Virginia.*

Pages 84/85: *Townspeople following the troops, Battle of Manassas reenactment, Virginia.* This page: *Jazz on the street, New Orleans, Louisiana.*

This page (above):
*Morning walk, Chatham
Square, Savannah,
Georgia.* This page
(below): *Vietnamese-
American fisherman,
Bayou La Batre, Alabama.*
Opposite page: *Hot air
balloon race, Greenville,
South Carolina.*

Opposite page:
*Retired farmer and wife
near Rocky Mount,
North Carolina.* This
page: *Third generation
steamboat captain
from Kentucky.*

WOODROW BLANKENSHIP Post Office Argo, Ky.

DRINK
Coca-Cola

DRINK
Pepsi-Cola

Have a Coke

Coca-Cola

Have a Coke

Coca-Cola

PEP

The Homeplace

A white frame country farmhouse sits securely harbored in the lee of a ridge of densely wooded hills. Its dark green shutters match the color of the painted tin roof. A wisp of blue-gray smoke curls from the stone chimney, spiraling slowly into the canopy of overhanging maples. From the front porch, the view is eastward across a broad field of hay, newly cut and baled. A dusty lane approaches the house circuitously, skirting the field and bordering on its opposite side a split rail fence and a woodlot, dark and quiet in the gathering dusk. The smell of hay and hickory smoke hangs in the air, pungent and familiar. An old dog trots forward to the edge of the yard to deliver a tail-wagging welcome, its bark like a friendly voice from the past. Across the length of the porch, the windows and front door throw out warm beams of mellow light. Voices and laughter float out into the evening air, echoing softly.

Home—coming back to the known, the comfortable, the safe, the secure—is an experience and a feeling of universal dimensions. All through history, around the world, people have been drawn by the magnetizing power of home. In the South, that power is reinforced by many influences—the primary importance of tradition and history, the binding ties of family relationships, the respect accorded to spiritual and social authority, the widely practiced and highly valued art of storytelling, the love of land, and the sense of place. Regardless of age, sex, race, or economic status, Southerners seldom can be indifferent to the feelings of duty, respect, kinship, and continuity that attach themselves to the image and reality of home.

The look of it is as diverse and varied in the mind's eye as are the people who summon it to remembrance. The country farmhouse is but one image among many: an antebellum mansion, a cabin in the woods, a weather-beaten coastal cottage, a bungalow on a shady small-town street, an urban town house, a surburban row house, a city apartment, a prefab, a mobile home—so many styles, and all of them with features duplicated elsewhere. It is not architecture that makes homeplaces in the South so distinctive, not physical characteristics or decorations or antiquity; rather, it is something in the mind and heart, something emotional.

Families, churches, schools, and towns periodically throw themselves into festive gatherings of their returning sons and daughters; in one recent year, an entire state, Tennessee, focused an abundance of time, money, and energy on a year-long homecoming celebration in which tens of thousands of people took part. Whatever it is that makes Southerners, religious or not, sing along to the strains of "Will the Circle Be Unbroken?" is also the force that beckons them back to their roots for periodic renewals of the faith and the promise. In cities and towns or in the country, from the mountains and hills to the bottomlands and the sea, home in the Southern experience is a fundamental feeling, a state of mind.

Pages 92/93: *Abandoned homeplace near Craig Springs, Virginia.* Pages 94/95: *Atlanta, Georgia.* Opposite page: *Rural post office, Argo, Kentucky.*

Close to sixty million people now live in the eleven Southern states framed by Virginia and Kentucky on the north and by Arkansas and Louisiana on the west. Until the end of World War II, when the population was only half as large as it is now, a substantial majority of the people lived in small towns or in the countryside. No cities of a million residents existed in the region, and only one or two were even half that large. Today, Atlanta leads five Southern metropolises in the million-plus class, and about twenty cities in the region have a half-million or more residents. Fully one-fourth of the hundred largest cities in the nation are in the eleven Southern states.

In just a little more than a generation, the South has been converted from a rural to a predominantly urban culture, and urbanization has made the region seem more uniform, more like the rest of the country. But the cities still retain some vestiges of a recognizable Southern character, and they also differ significantly one from another. Mere mention of about three dozen underscores the point.

Age and geography account for much of the variety. The ocean cities have been here the longest, of course— St. Augustine (the oldest), Savannah, Charleston, Wilmington, Norfolk—and they have about them a look and feel of

ageless grace. Pensacola and Mobile reflect the same charm in their outward facing toward the Gulf of Mexico. The younger cities of Tampa and St. Petersburg on the west coast of Florida, along with Jacksonville on the east, also look to the sea.

New Orleans gets much of its personality from its status as both a seaport and a river city. Inland, the river ports of Baton Rouge and Memphis on the Mississippi, Louisville on the Ohio, Nashville on the Cumberland, and Richmond on the James all can trace long histories of growth up from the waterfront. Rivers are also important to the geography and history of Little Rock, Chattanooga, Knoxville, and Columbia, but other physical features—hills, mountains, and plains—seem somehow closer to their nature. Asheville and Roanoke are truly mountain cities, while several others—Lexington and Birmingham, Greenville and Spartanburg, Greensboro and Winston-Salem—circle the mountain periphery.

This page: *Yard work, Orton Plantation near Wilmington, North Carolina.* Opposite page: *Porches in Charleston, South Carolina.*

98

Florida's explosive growth (its population has quadrupled since 1950) virtually has created several cities from scratch. In 1900, Miami was a swampy village of a few hundred people, and Fort Lauderdale did not exist at all; now, both are hubs of metropolitan areas that number more than a million people. Orlando is yet another of the Sunshine State's "new" cities. Finally, between the mountains and the sea, the South is spotted with thriving capital cities such as Jackson and Montgomery and Raleigh, budding metropolises such as Charlotte, and the prototype urban center of them all, the one and only Atlanta.

In these thirty-six cities live about twenty million people—one-third of the entire population of the region. As cities everywhere become more and more alike, what do the ones in the South still have in common, and what basic characteristics still give them recognition as Southern places? One thing is the climate, especially the hot and humid summers. Another is the pace of life—not as slow and deliberate as it once was, certainly, but still not as brisk and frenzied as is the pace in the cities of the North. There is a more personal atmosphere, too, marked by friendliness and intimacy (or is it simply curiosity?) in the day-to-day dealings of casual acquaintances and even strangers.

"Atlanta (read Nashville, Charlotte, Tampa, etc.) is just an overgrown country town," the familiar line goes. Nobody says that about Boston, New York, Chicago, or Los Angeles. The Southern cities still take pride in their rural origins, even though the connections have become weaker and more fragile in the modern age.

Meanwhile, out in the real Southern countryside, small-town and rural living is undergoing changes just as profound and as pervasive as those taking place in the cities. The family farm is disappearing, losing out to mechanized superfarms which are larger in size and fewer in number. Manufacturing and service industries are the main employers now—they and the federal, state, county, and municipal governments. Southerners from the country are moving into the towns and cities, looking for work—and at the same time, many urban dwellers, weary of the frenetic pace of life on the avenues, are driving up and down the backroads, searching for country homes and a little tranquility.

Addresses change, and so do ways of living; old domestic habits must yield to new necessities, new preferences. There was a time not so long ago when families sat down together to eat two or three meals a day, but that is an anachronism now. Other activities ranging from religion and education to shopping and entertainment have been equally as affected, as Southern society moves to the threshold of the twenty-first century.

Still, in the homeplaces themselves, tradition is as ever-present and visible as a member of the family, and contemporary living is accented by daily remembrance of things past. Now, as always, signs of the real South, the good South, come shining through: human comedy and drama, words and music, food and drink, manners and rituals, kin and friends, birth and marriage, death and burial. It is in the homeplace, as much as anywhere else, that Southern history is told, remembered, preserved, and sometimes made. The land and the homeplace are extensions of each other, permanently and inseparably linked.

In the frame house, the mansion, the cabin, Southerners cling to myth and history, and sometimes the two seem virtually identical. The Southern homeplace—city, town, and country— is both a repository of the past and a seedbed of the future. The connection between the two was one of William Faulkner's central themes. "In the South," he once said, "the past is never dead. It's not even past."

Opposite page:
Chippewa Square,
Savannah, Georgia.

Pages 102/103: *The Battery, Charleston, South Carolina.* Pages 104/105: *The Kentucky Derby at Churchill Downs, Louisville, Kentucky.* This page: *St. Charles Streetcar line, New Orleans, Louisiana.* Opposite page: *The High Museum, Atlanta, Georgia.*

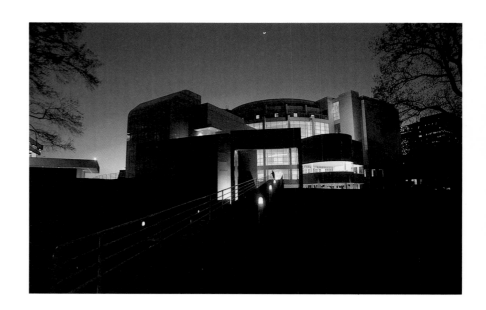

Opposite page:
*Country girl,
Morganton, North
Carolina.* This
page: *Roadside
stand near Sperryville,
Virginia.*

Pages 110/111: *Nashville,
Tennessee.* Opposite
page: *Mountain wedding,
Cashiers, North Carolina.*
This page (above):
*Returning from chores,
Celo Community, North
Carolina.* This page
(below): *Hand painted
road sign, Celo Commuity,
North Carolina.*

REV. MARTIN LUTHER KING, JR.
1929 — 1968
"Free at last, Free at last,
Thank God Almighty
I'm Free at last."

Pages 114/115: *Martin Luther King, Jr., Memorial, Atlanta, Georgia.* This page: *Home of Thomas Jefferson, Monticello, Charlottesville, Virginia.* Opposite page: *The Oakleigh House, Mobile, Alabama.*

Opposite page: *The
Cupola House, circa 1725,
Edenton, North Carolina.*
This page: *Garden shed,
Rosedown Plantation,
St. Francisville, Louisiana.*

Pages 120/121: *Callaway Gardens, Pine Mountain, Georgia.* Opposite page: *One of the oldest residents, Leary, Georgia.* This page (above): *Swamp woman, Okefenokee Swamp, Georgia.* This page (below): *Cherokee Indian craftsman and artist, Cherokee, North Carolina.*

Pages 124/125: *Late afternoon in Ty Ty, Georgia.* This page: *Mountain church near Johnson City, Tennessee.* Opposite page: *Pisgah National Forest near Sunburst, North Carolina.*

Acknowledgements

My debt is great indeed to the many people and institutions who have assisted me in the planning and production of this book. No successful project that covers this much territory over such a long period of time can be the product of a solitary effort.

I am very much obliged to Bob and Lee Anderson for their thoughts on the structure of the book and in helping to select the author. I am also grateful to Oliver and Lisa Houck for their enthusiastic help in planning my coverage of their region and for giving me shelter when needed.

I am deeply indebted to Dick Durrance II and Steve Uzzell III for their tireless editorial assistance and strong personal support. I was also very fortunate to have the assistance of Mark Schifrin, who gave so much of himself when it was needed most.

My deep gratitude goes to the Citizens and Southern Banks, a financial institution with roots firmly planted in Southern soil and with an abiding appreciation of the South and the people who live and work there. Their initial interest led to a generous grant which makes this book possible. I was pleased and honored to work closely with the C&S staff in several states. A very special thank you goes to John Haynie, Jr., and to Enoch Prow, as well as to Mr. Bennett Brown who is chairman of C&S for their trust in my vision and their words of encouragement along the way.

A special word of thanks goes to the National Geographic Society and to Bill Garrett, editor, for their permission to use some of the images I produced on earlier assignments for them south of the Mason-Dixon line.

Along the way I was supported by many people who gave graciously of their time, energy, and knowledge. I would like to give a very special thanks to Orissa Arend and John Schenken, Ben Chapman, Ron Comedy, Dana Contratto, John Crawford and Kathy Sakas, Ralph and Nonnie Daniel, Kim Davidson, Jacques DePuy, Scott and Beth Glass, Critt Graham, Greg and Bubbles Guirard, Panos Kammenos, Rob Kennedy, Sue Lyons and Mark Lyons, Jorge Mora, Dick and Joyce Murlless and the wonderful staff at Wilderness Southeast, David Pearson and Chris Pearson, Wallace Street, Charles C. Wilkes, Patricia Young of the Delta Queen Steamship Company, and the many others.

My two assistants during the production phases were Peter Wu and John Mullin. As the miles and days went by, they supported me with their good ideas, strong backs, and high energy. Without the support and friendship of Peter and John, I could never have hoped to cover so much in so little time.

When all the photos were made and it came time to design the book, I relied entirely on the extraordinary good taste and fine design of Bob Cargill and Art Riser of Cargill and Associates, Inc. in Atlanta. Bob, Art, and their talented staff, especially Pam Eitzen, performed the delicate task of designing the book with consummate skill, remarkable patience, and old-fashioned graciousness. I shall long be in their debt.

A very special debt must be acknowledged to my office manager and colleague, Shelley Yerman, who kept the fort going in my long absences and did a yeoman's job on all the necessary typing and collecting of the book parts.

My hat is also off to Jean Andrews of Graphic Arts Center Publishing Company for her outstanding editing and organizational efforts. Her superior command of the English language as well as her long suffering patience made her efforts critical to the book's success. Doug Pfeiffer, my editor at Graphic Arts Center Publishing Company, has proven to be an excellent book producer. His suggestions were always right on the mark.

It was a pleasure to get to know and to work with John Egerton, the sensitive and insightful writer of the literary side of the book. He responded to the pressures and tight deadlines with special grace and silent determination during a difficult time of his life. I am honored to share these pages with him.

Last, but perhaps most important, I say a special thanks to my wife, Prisca, my son, Will, and my daughter, Prisca. As the days became weeks and then months, it has been their special sense of togetherness and purpose that has unified us all. They were often with me on the road, and when not physically so, their love and spirit sustained me.

— *Bill Weems*